LIFE IN THE REPUBLIC OF TEXAS

John Wimberly

Spotlight on TEXAS™

Rosen Classroom™

New York

Published in 2010 by The Rosen Publishing Group, Inc.
29 East 21st Street, New York, NY 10010

Book Design: Daniel Hosek

Photo Credits: Cover, pp. 3, 4, 6, 8, 10, 14, 18, 20, 22, 24, 26, 28, 30, 31, 32 (Texas emblem on all), pp. 3–32 (textured background), 28 (flag), back cover (Texas flag) Shutterstock.com; cover (top background), p.7 courtesy Texas State Library and Archives Commission; cover (flag), pp. 8, 10 (map), 23 (top), 27 (top) Wikimedia Commons; cover (Sam Houston), pp. 6 (Santa Anna), 15 (Sam Houston), courtesy Library of Congress; cover (bottom background), p. 20 (Comanches), George Caitlin/The Bridgeman Art Library/Getty Images; p. 5 © GeoAtlas; p. 9 Architect of the Capitol; p. 11 (ships) Peter Harholdt/SuperStock/Getty Images; pp. 12 (Henry Smith), 16–17 (battle), 19 (Lamar) The State Preservation Board, Austin, Texas; pp. 21 (Parker), 27 (bottom) Hulton Archive/Getty Images; p. 23 (bottom) Don Klumpp/Getty Images; p. 25 USTA's Institute of Texan Cultures, #068-0185; Courtesy of James P. Prowell.

Library of Congress Cataloging-in-Publication Data

Wimberley, John, 1945-
Life in the Republic of Texas / John Wimberley.
p. cm. — (Spotlight on Texas)
Includes index.
ISBN 978-1-61532-469-9 (pbk.)
ISBN 978-1-61532-470-5
ISBN 978-1-61532-471-2 (library binding)
1. Texas—History—Republic, 1836-1846—Juvenile literature. I. Title.
F390.W75 2010
976.4'04—dc22

2009050712

Manufactured in the United States of America

CPSIA Compliance Information: Batch # WW10RC: For further information contact Rosen Publishing, New York, New York at 1-800-237-9932.

Contents

Texas Before the Republic

To understand life in the **Republic** of Texas (1836–1845), we need to know something about Texas history. What was life like before the republic? What events led to the creation of the republic?

Before Europeans came, Texas was home to native peoples who had lived in the area for thousands of years. Spain claimed the land in the 1500s. Spanish **missionaries** founded **missions** to bring their faith, language, and way of life to the area's Native Americans.

In this book, we'll look at Texas history and some of the events, ideas, and leaders that shaped life in the republic.

The First Towns

The Spanish missions were the first European settlements in Texas. Many Native Americans were part of the communities. Towns grew around the missions as American and Spanish farmers, ranchers, tradesmen, soldiers, and merchants moved in. In the 1700s, José de Escandón, a Spanish governor, founded several missions and over twenty towns in the area around the Rio Grande. He is often called the "father" of the lower Rio Grande valley.

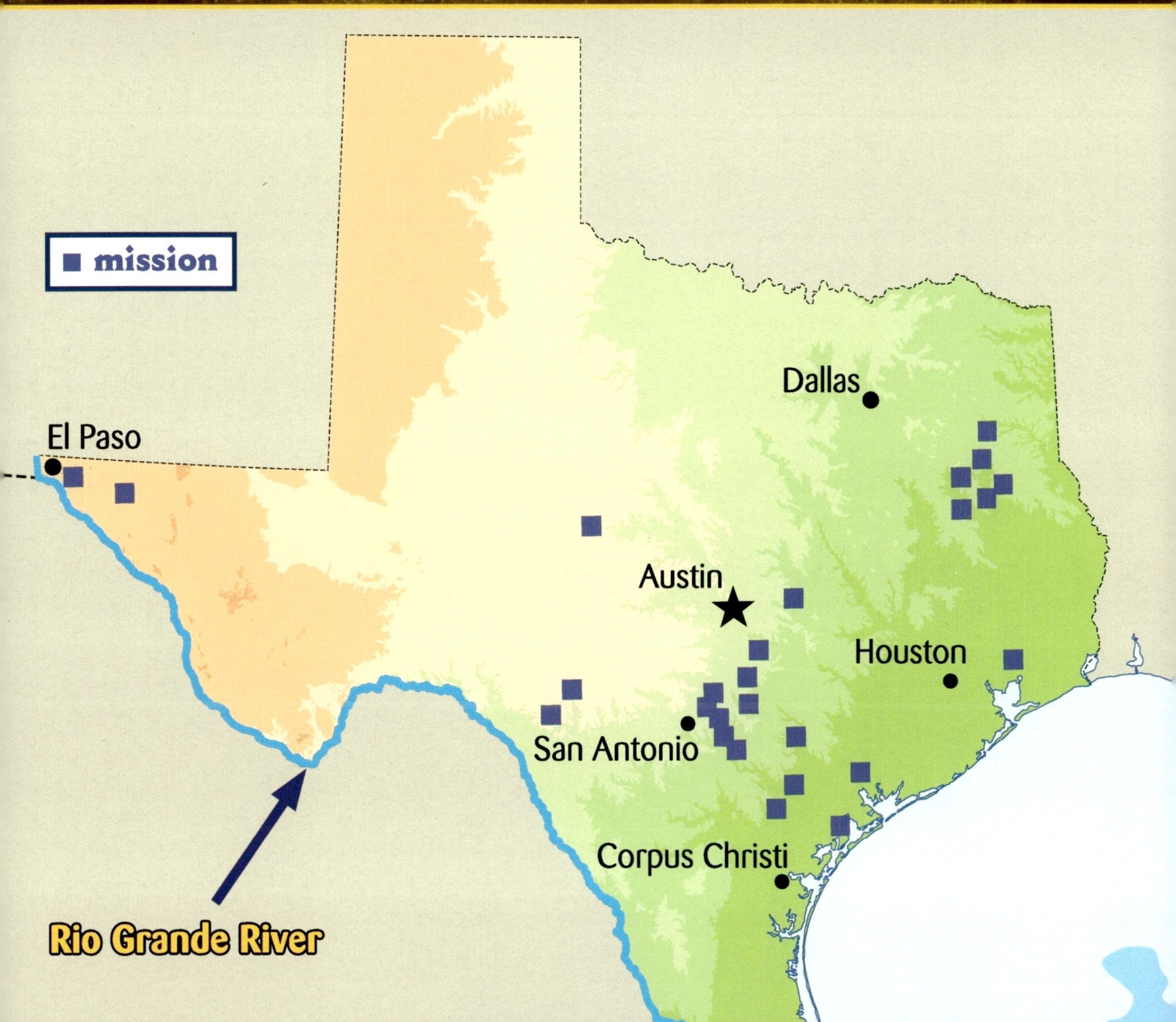

This map shows Spanish missions in Texas from 1659 to 1795.

SPANISH AND MEXICAN TEXAS

For centuries, Spain ruled an area in North America called New Spain. It included modern Mexico and much of Texas and the southwestern United States.

In the early 1800s, settlers in the area were unhappy with Spanish rule. They wanted independence. The Mexican War of Independence (1810–1821) was fought. The new nation of Mexico was created in 1821.

The Mexican government wanted people to settle on its lands. It welcomed settlers from America and European countries to the newly created Mexican states, including Coahuila (koh-ah-WEE-lah) and Texas.

The Mexican states elected their own leaders and governed themselves. That changed when Antonio López de Santa Anna became president of Mexico in 1833.

Santa Anna

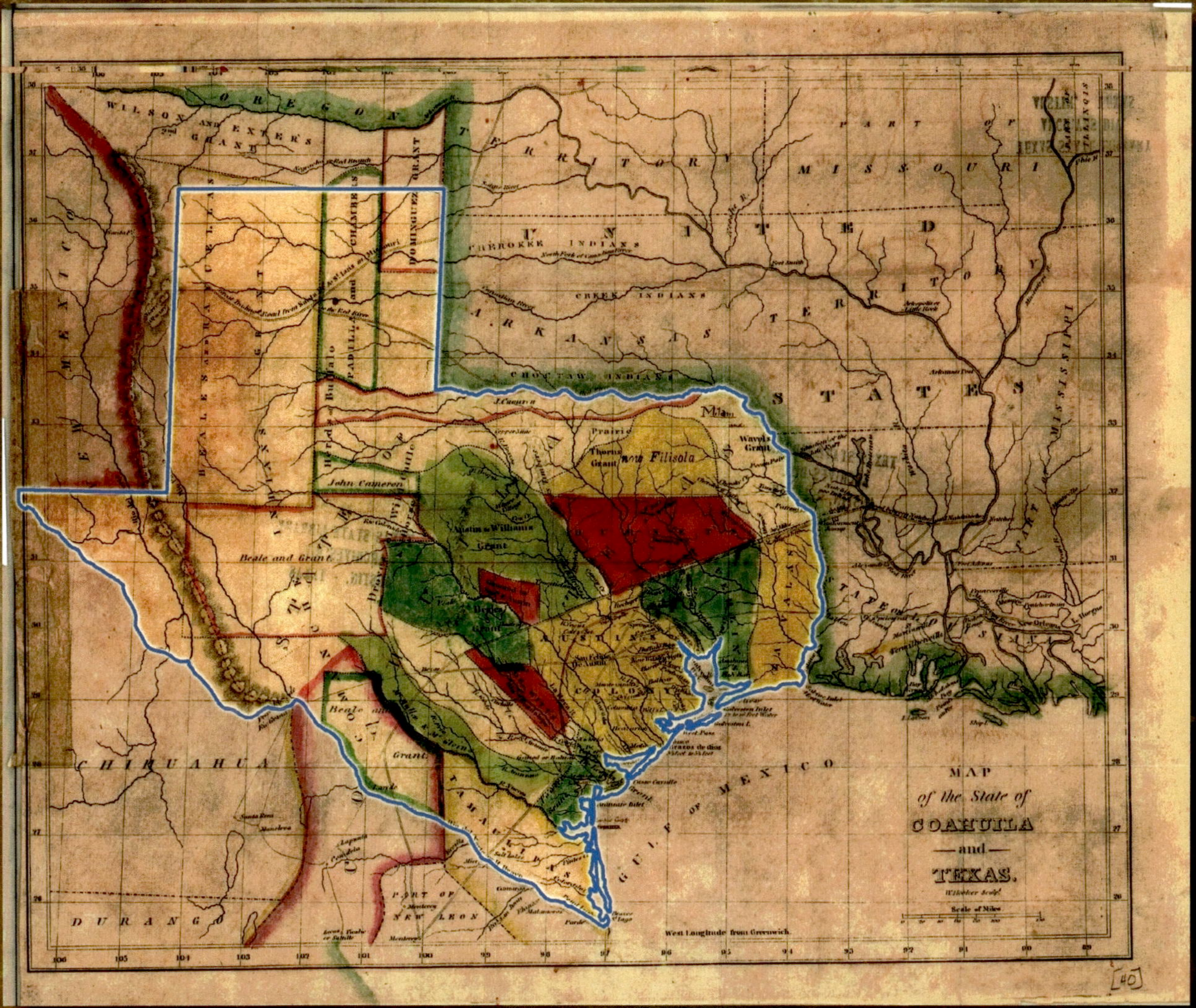

Modern-day Texas is outlined on this 1833 map of Coahuila and Texas.

The Texas Revolution

The Texas **Revolution** (1835–1836) began after unhappiness about Santa Anna's rule spread throughout Mexico. In Texas, some **Anglo** and Mexican leaders wanted power returned to the Mexican states. Others wanted total independence from Mexico. Many battles between the Mexican army and Texas settlers took place. On March 2, 1836, Texas leaders signed the Texas Declaration of Independence. The Republic of Texas was officially established. Texas won the revolution on April 21, 1836. The Republic of Texas became a free and separate country.

The Battle of Gonzales was the first battle of the Texas Revolution. This flag was painted by two women from the town. They wanted to lift the spirits of the town's fighters and to tease and anger the Mexican troops.

The "Father of Texas"

Stephen F. Austin is known as the "Father of Texas." In 1822, he founded the first American colony in Texas. Much of the colony's success was because of his direction and hard work. He was the connection between the Mexican government and the settlers. He strongly backed Texas independence from Mexico.

THE REPUBLIC OF TEXAS

Under Mexican rule, the government was far away. Settlers lived the way they wanted to—keeping themselves safe, growing crops, raising animals, and working in their communities.

However, after Texas became independent, many more Europeans and Americans settled there. These ranchers, farmers, tradesmen, and merchants wanted a say in how they were governed. They elected leaders whose ideas, beliefs, and actions shaped life in the republic.

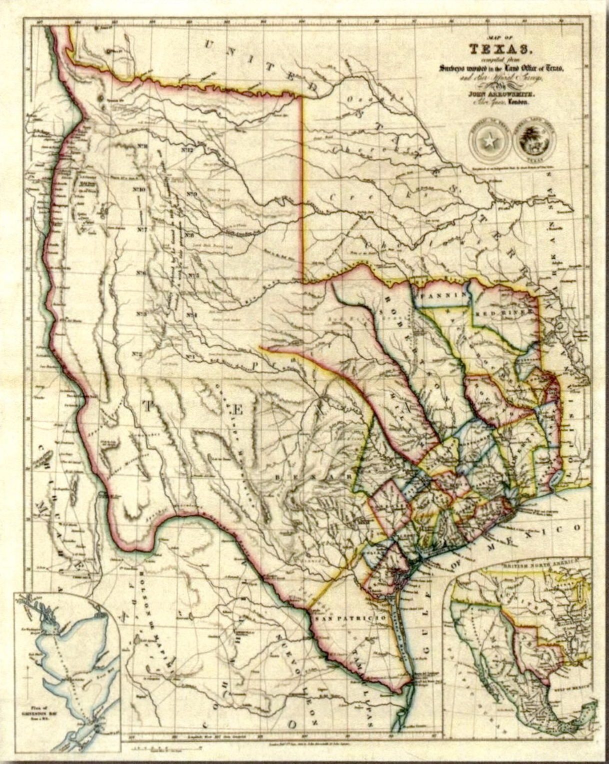

This map shows the area governed by the Republic of Texas in 1843.

The Texas Navy

Texas has a long coastline. During the revolution, the Texas navy had four ships to guard the coast against Mexican attacks. By 1837, three of them were sunk or captured. The fourth was sold because Texas couldn't pay to have it fixed. In 1839, the republic bought six ships. The navy guarded Texas from Mexico. It guarded waterways for supplies. The navy also seized ships and captured their goods to get money for the republic.

Sailing ships like the schooner pictured above were used by the Texas navy.

The Republic of Texas faced many problems. It didn't have much money. It had continuing struggles with Mexico. It didn't have strong ties with other countries. There were many disagreements about Native Americans, the size of the republic, and how it should be governed. Texans had two main points of view. Some wanted to remove Native Americans from the area, spread the republic west to the Pacific Ocean, and remain an independent nation. Others wanted to make peace with the Native Americans, keep Texas the same size, and become part of the United States.

Henry Smith was governor of Texas during the early stages of the Texas Revolution.

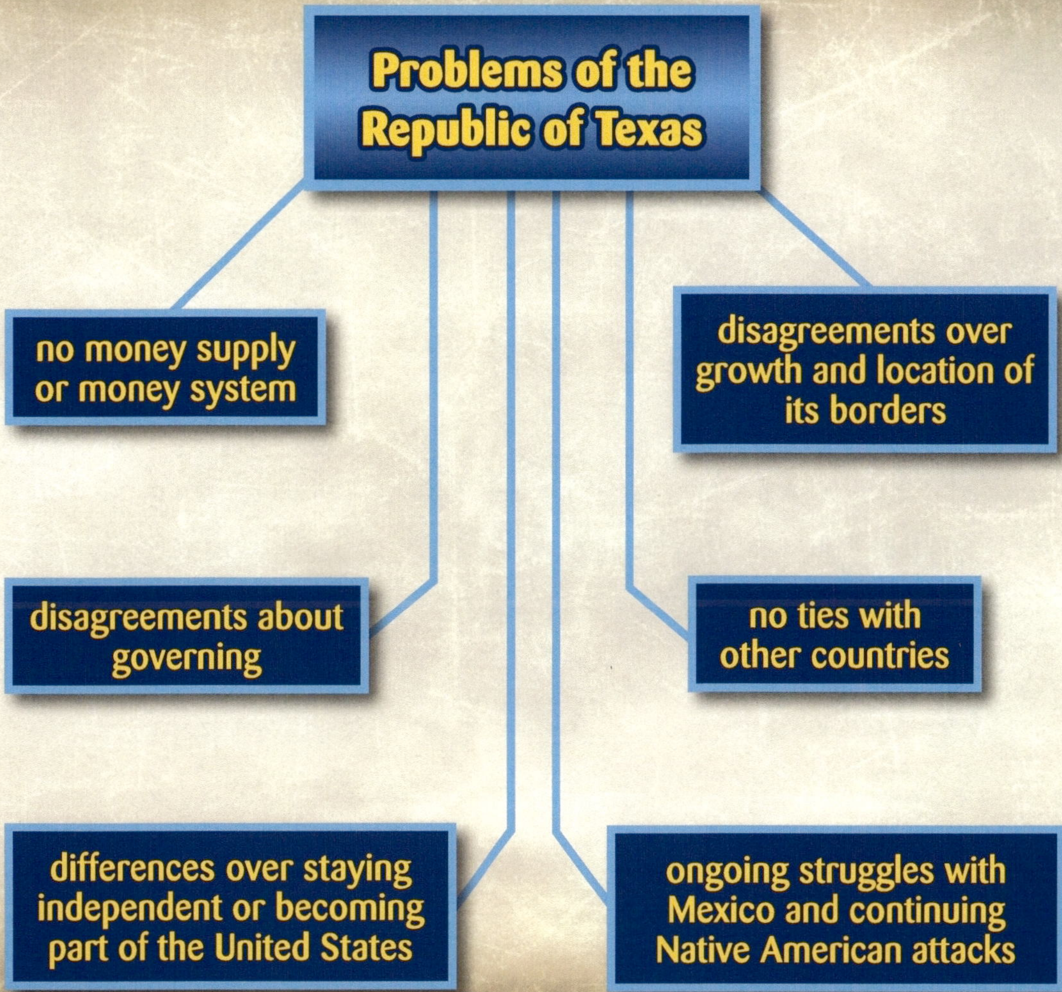
Problems of the Republic of Texas
no money supply or money system
disagreements over growth and location of its borders
disagreements about governing
no ties with other countries
differences over staying independent or becoming part of the United States
ongoing struggles with Mexico and continuing Native American attacks

Sam Houston

Samuel (Sam) Houston was a leader in the Republic of Texas. He was born in Virginia and moved to Tennessee at the age of 13. When he was about 16, he left his family and lived among the Cherokee Indians. Houston grew to understand and respect the Cherokees. He loved the freedom of their way of life and learned to live like a native.

Houston left the Cherokees after 3 years and joined the U.S. Army. He fought with bravery and skill during the **War of 1812**. After he was wounded, he left the army and studied law. He ran for public office and was elected to the U.S. Congress. Later, he became governor of Tennessee. Personal problems caused him to leave his position as governor. Once again, he went to live among the Cherokees.

This is an 1856 picture of Sam Houston. He is considered one of the most important people involved with the Republic of Texas.

In 1832, Houston left the Cherokees and moved to Texas. He believed in the fight for Texas independence from Mexico. He joined the Texas army and fought in the revolution. Houston commanded the troops during the last battle of the revolution. He played a major role in founding the Republic of Texas.

The Battle of San Jacinto (1836) was the last battle of the Texas Revolution. Sam Houston and his soldiers beat Santa Anna and the Mexican army.

Sam Houston was a respected leader. In 1836, he was elected the republic's first president. He was reelected as its third president in 1841. Houston guided the new nation through many problems. He believed in law and order. He worked to build the **economy** and settle differences with Native Americans and the Mexican government. He wanted the Republic of Texas to become part of the United States.

Mirabeau B. Lamar

Mirabeau B. Lamar, another important leader in the Republic of Texas, also fought in the Texas army during the revolution. He became **secretary of war** when the republic was first founded. He later served as Sam Houston's vice president. Lamar was elected the second president of the republic in 1838 because Houston couldn't serve two terms in a row.

As president, Lamar continued some of the work Houston had begun. He wanted to keep law and order. He built ties with other nations and worked to improve the economy. He suggested a national bank and worked to set up public schools.

Lamar disagreed with Houston about several things. He wanted the republic to remain independent. He tried unsuccessfully to get settlers in other Mexican states to join the republic. He wanted to drive out Native Americans.

This is a picture of Mirabeau Lamar. He was president of the Republic of Texas from 1838 to 1841.

Native Americans in the Republic

As settlers continued to move to Texas, they needed more and more land to grow crops, raise animals, and build towns. Many native peoples lived by hunting, fishing, gathering plants, or farming. They were pushed off their lands and forced to change their ways of life. Fighting between settlers and Native American tribes such as Kiowas, Apaches, Tonkawas, Cherokees, and Comanches increased.

This is an 1834 painting of Comanche fighters riding into battle.

Native Americans had occupied the **Great Plains** for centuries. Anger and struggles between settlers and Native Americans grew stronger when support increased for removing Native Americans by force. Disagreements, dishonesty, and broken promises increased the attacks.

Chief Quanah Parker, the last Comanche chief, tried unsuccessfully to help his people continue their way of life.

The Comanches, who lived mostly in the northern parts of Texas, didn't want settlers on their lands. As a result, there were many attacks and wars between the republic and the Comanches.

The Texas Rangers

The first Texas Rangers were men hired by Stephen Austin in 1823 to "range" over the area and guard his colony. In 1835, they were made official by Texas leaders. They patrolled and guarded settlements against Native American attacks. During the Texas Revolution, they acted as scouts and message carriers.

Texas didn't have money for a regular army, so it was the Rangers—along with **volunteers** and **militia**—who guarded against Native American and Mexican dangers. During Mirabeau Lamar's presidency, the Rangers were used to drive Cherokees and Comanches out of the republic.

This statue of a Texas Ranger was constructed in 1907. It stands outside the Texas State Capitol in Austin.

The Oldest Force

Captain John Coffee "Jack" Hays led the Texas Rangers in the 1840s. He had the Rangers adopt the revolver—a gun that didn't need to be loaded after each shot. The Texas Rangers are the oldest state law force in North America. Today, they're considered Texas's most highly trained law officers.

The "Mother of Texas"

In 1820, Jane Wilkinson Long became one of the first Anglo women to settle in Texas. Life wasn't easy. Travel was slow. Weather could be unpleasant. There were unfamiliar animals and bugs. Fresh food and health care were often lacking. Life outside settlements could be very lonely.

Jane's husband believed in the fight for Texas independence. He was away for long periods of time. Jane, her young daughter, and a servant were often alone.

After her husband was killed, Jane left Texas. She returned in 1824. She lived in a town in Stephen Austin's colony and earned a living through farming and renting out rooms in her home. Her life is an example of the spirit, bravery, and strength of the women who lived in the Republic of Texas. Jane Long is often called the "Mother of Texas."

This is an oil painting of Jane Wilkinson Long.

Mexican Women

Mexican women helped shape society and ways of life in Texas from its beginning through the time of the republic.

Women from other states in Mexico made the long, tiring, hard journey north to settle in Texas. Many settled around the missions with their families. Their husbands were farmers, craftsmen, and soldiers. These women helped with the farmwork, prepared food, and took care of farm animals. They also made items such as candles, soap, and clothing that were used by their families and the community. The women often treated people in the settlement who were hurt or sick. Some Mexican women married Anglos, mixing their practices with others in the communities.

This picture shows a cutaway of a mid-1800s farm cabin. The cabin has one room that served as the kitchen, living, and sleeping area. Bathrooms were outside the cabin. Water had to be brought to the cabin from wells like the one you see to the right of the cabin.

Honor and Recognition

Patricia de la Garza De León settled in southwestern Texas in the 1800s with her husband. In 1824, they established a mostly Mexican community on land they received after Mexico became independent from Spain. Patricia helped set up a school and church. She continued Spanish and Mexican practices in the republic. She supported the independence movement in Texas. What she did for the republic was recognized by the State of Texas with this historic marker.

The Republic Ends

Life in the Republic of Texas was shaped by the rule of Spain and Mexico and by the needs, beliefs, and ideas of the individuals who settled there. Though the republic lasted less than 10 years, the strength, courage, and spirit of its people helped form modern-day Texas.

The Lone Star State

Texas became part of the United States in 1845. The Texas state flag has been used since 1839, when it flew over the Republic of Texas. Texas is known as the "Lone Star State" because of the single white star on its flag. Some say the single star stands for the idea that Texas was strong enough to stand by itself.

Life in the Republic of Texas

1822	Stephen Austin founds first American colony in Texas.
1823	Stephen Austin hires the first Texas Rangers.
1835	Texas Revolution begins. Texas Rangers become official.
1836	Texas Declaration of Independence is signed. Republic of Texas is created. Texas creates a navy. Texas Revolution ends.
1836	Samuel Houston is elected first president of the republic.
1838	Mirabeau Lamar is elected second president of the republic.
1839	Lone Star flag becomes official. Six ships become the republic's navy.
1841	Samuel Houston is reelected president of the republic.
1845	Texas becomes part of the United States.

Reader Response Projects

- The painting on pages 16 and 17 shows the Battle of San Jacinto. Research the battle on the Internet. Write a news report describing the action. Be sure to include who, what, when, where, and why.

- Imagine that you live in the Republic of Texas. Choose a type of settler or a person you have read about in this book. Do research on the Internet. Use facts you find to write a journal entry that tells who you are, what you do, and what your daily life is like.

- Choose one chapter from the book. Write an outline of important points you would use to summarize the chapter for another student.

- The Republic of Texas existed from 1836–1845. Using this book, the Internet, and other sources, create a poster that shows how the republic affected life in modern-day Texas.

GLOSSARY

Anglo (ANG-gloh) A white, non-Hispanic person.

economy (ih-KAH-nuh-mee) The use of money and goods.

Great Plains (GRAYT PLAYNZ) A large, grassland area of central North America.

militia (muh-LIH-shuh) A group of citizens who aren't soldiers but are trained and ready to fight if needed.

mission (MIH-shun) A place where people teach their faith and way of life to those in the area.

missionary (MIH-shuh-nehr-ee) A person sent to work in a mission.

republic (rih-PUH-blihk) A type of government where people elect leaders to make laws and run the country.

revolution (reh-vuh-LOO-shun) A fight against the government in place.

secretary of war (SEH-kruh-tehr-ee UHV WOHR) The person in charge of guarding a country.

volunteer (vah-luhn-TIHR) A person who offers to do something.

War of 1812 (WOHR UHV 1812) A war between the United States and Britain that began in 1812 and ended in 1815.

INDEX

Due to the changing nature of Internet links, the Rosen Publishing Group, Inc., has developed an online list of Web sites related to the subject of this book. This site is updated regularly. Please use this link to access the list: **http://www.rcbmlinks.com/sot/reptex/**